Contents

The Basics

The Parts of the Trumpet

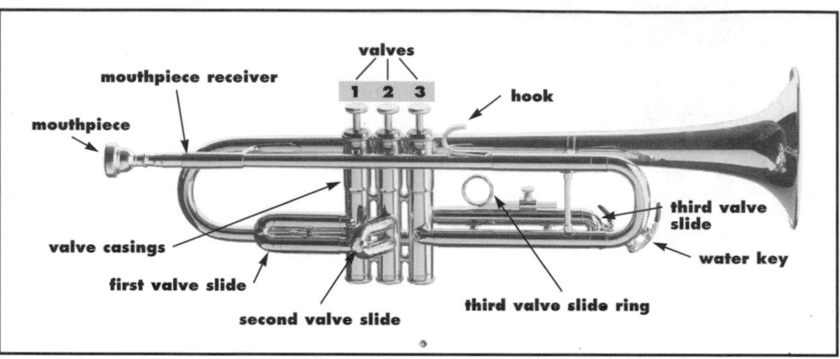

Posture

Whether sitting on the edge of your chair or standing, you should always keep your:

- Spine straight and tall,
- Shoulders back and relaxed, and
- Feet flat on the floor.

Breathing & Air Stream

Breathing is a natural thing we all do constantly, but you must control your breathing while playing the trumpet. To discover the correct air stream to play your trumpet:

- Place the palm of your hand near your mouth.
- Inhale deeply through the corners of your mouth, keeping your shoulders steady. Your waist should expand like a balloon.
- Whisper "tah" as you gradually exhale a stream of air into your palm.

The air you feel is the air stream. It produces sound through the instrument. Your tongue is like a faucet or valve that releases or stops the air stream.

Your First Tone

Your mouth's position on the instrument is called the embouchure (ahm' bah shure). Developing a good embouchure takes time and effort, so carefully follow these beginning steps:

- Moisten your lips and bring them together as if saying the letter "m."
- Relax your jaw, separating your upper and lower teeth.
- Form a slightly puckered smile to firm the corners of your mouth.
- Direct a full air stream through the center of your lips, creating a buzz. (You should buzz frequently without your mouthpiece.)
- While forming your "buzzing" embouchure, center the mouthpiece on your lips.
- Take in a full breath through the corners of your mouth and start your buzz with the syllable "tah." Your tongue will act like a valve, opening up the stream of air. Buzz through the center of your lips and try to keep the sound steady and even. This will probably feel very strange and even silly to you at first, but this buzzing is *the* fundamental sound of all brass instruments.

Reading Music

Musical sounds are indicated by symbols called ***notes*** written on a ***staff***. Notes come in several forms, but every note indicates ***pitch*** and ***rhythm***.

The Staff

Music Staff

The ***music staff*** has 5 lines and 4 spaces where notes and rests are written.

Ledger Lines

Ledger lines extend the music staff. Notes on ledger lines can be above or below the staff.

Measures & Bar Lines

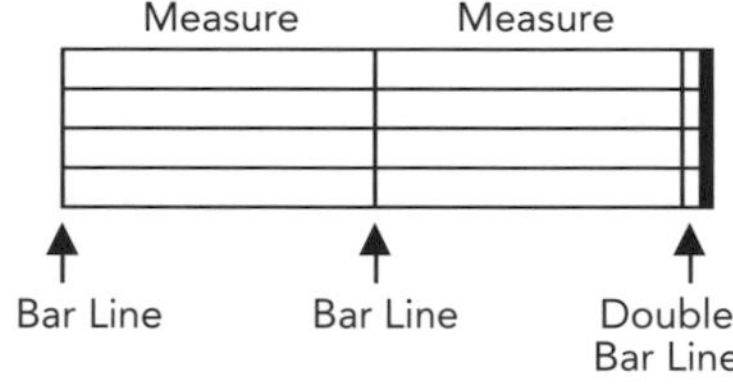

Bar lines divide the music staff into ***measures.***
The ***Double Bar*** indicates the end of a piece of music.

Treble Clef
(G Clef) indicates the position of note names on a music staff: Second line is G.

Time Signature
indicates how many beats per measure and what kind of note gets one beat.

= **4 beats** per measure
= **Quarter note** gets one beat

Pitch

Pitch (the highness or lowness of a note) is indicated by the horizontal placement of the note on the staff. Notes higher on the staff are higher in pitch; notes lower on the staff are lower in pitch. To name the pitches, we use the first seven letters of the alphabet: A, B, C, D, E, F, and G. The ***treble clef*** (𝄞) assigns a particular pitch name to each line and space on the staff, centered around the pitch G, located on the second line of the staff. Music for the trumpet is always written in the treble clef. (Some instruments may make use of other clefs, which make the lines and spaces represent different pitches.)

Note Names

Each note is on a line or space of the staff. These note names are indicated by the Treble Clef.

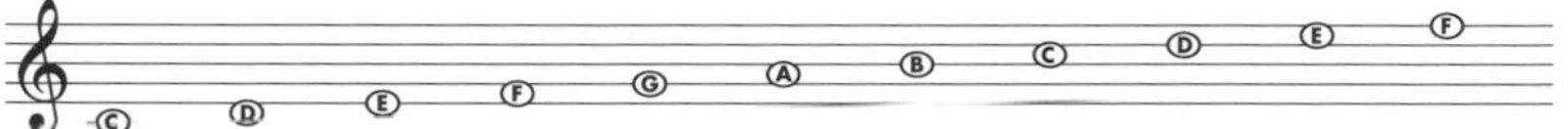

Sharps, Flats, and Naturals

These musical symbols are called accidentals which raise or lower the pitch of a note.

Sharp ♯ raises the note and remains in effect for the entire measure.

Flat ♭ lowers the note and remains in effect for the entire measure.

Natural ♮ cancels a flat (♭) or sharp (♯) and remains in effect for the entire measure.

Rhythm

Rhythm refers to how long, or for how many ***beats*** a note lasts. The beat is the pulse of music, and like your heartbeat it usually remains very steady. To help keep track of the beats in a piece of music, the staff is divided into ***measures***. The ***time signature*** (numbers such as $\frac{4}{4}$ or $\frac{6}{8}$ at the beginning of the staff) indicates how many beats you will find in each measure. Counting the beats or tapping your foot can help to maintain a steady beat. Tap you foot down on each beat and up on each "&."

$\frac{4}{4}$ Time

Count:	1	&	2	&	3	&	4	&
Tap:	↓	↑	↓	↑	↓	↑	↓	↑

$\frac{4}{4}$ is probably the most common time signature. The ***top number*** tells you how many beats are in each measure; the ***bottom number*** tells you what kind of note receives one beat. In $\frac{4}{4}$ time there are four beats in the measure and a ***quarter note*** (♩ or ♩) equals one beat.

> **4** = **4 beats** per measure
> **4** = **Quarter note** gets one beat

Assembling Your Trumpet

- Hold the trumpet with your left hand. Your thumb and your fingers should grasp the instrument around the valve casings. Put your left ring finger inside the third valve slide ring. (Refer to the picture under "The Parts of the Trumpet.")
- Hold the mouthpiece at the wide end with your right hand. Gently twist the mouthpiece into the mouthpiece receiver. Never pound the mouthpiece in. It can get stuck, and you will need special equipment (called a "mouthpiece puller") to get it out without damaging your trumpet.

How to Hold Your Trumpet

- Arch your right hand to form a backwards "C." Rest your right thumb alongside the first valve casing under the straight tube that leads to the mouthpiece. Your fingers will rest on the three valves, with your little finger resting on the *top* of the hook. Don't try to support the trumpet with your right hand. The left hand will hold the weight of the instrument and the right hand will merely help balance it.
- Always sit or stand tall when playing. Hold the trumpet as shown:

Putting Away Your Instrument

- Blow air through the trumpet while opening the water key(s) to empty any condensation from the instrument.
- Remove the mouthpiece and put it in the appropriate place in your case. Once a week, wash the mouthpiece with warm tap water and dry thoroughly.
- Wipe off your trumpet with a clean, soft cloth. Return the instrument to its case.
- Occasionally your slides will need greasing. Obtain special slide grease from your music dealer.
- You should oil your valves regularly. Only use specially-made valve oil, which should be available from your musical instrument dealer. To oil your trumpet valves:
- Unscrew the valve at the top of the valve casing and lift the valve half-way out.
- Apply a few drops of valve oil to the exposed valve.
- Carefully return the valve into its casing. It will only fit one way, and the top of the valve should easily screw back into place once it is properly inserted.

Lesson 1

Track 1

The First Note: G

G is played "open" that is, with no valves pressed. Rest your fingers on the valves, relaxed and curved. Many different notes can be played open on the trumpet, so match your pitch to the CD.

Notes and Rests

Music uses symbols to indicated both the length of sound and of silence. Symbols indicating sound are called **Notes**. Symbols indicating silence are called **Rests**.

Whole Note/Whole Rest

A whole note means to play for four full beats (a complete measure in $\frac{4}{4}$ time). A whole rest means to be silent for four full beats.

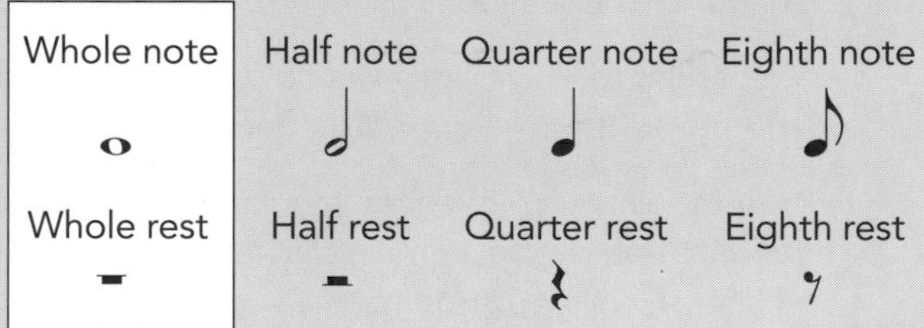

Listen to recorded track on the CD, then play along. Try to match the sound on the recording.

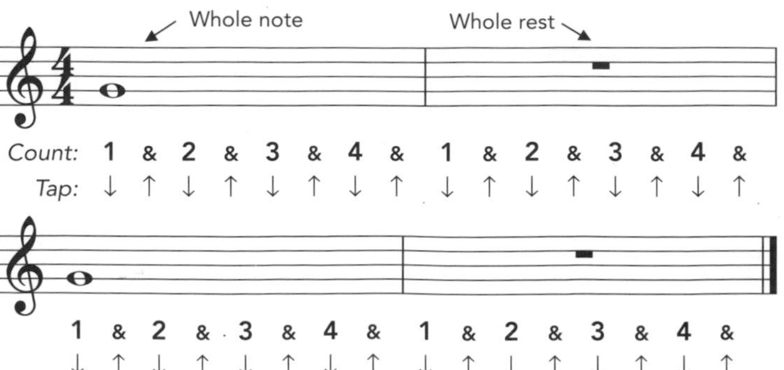

Count and Play

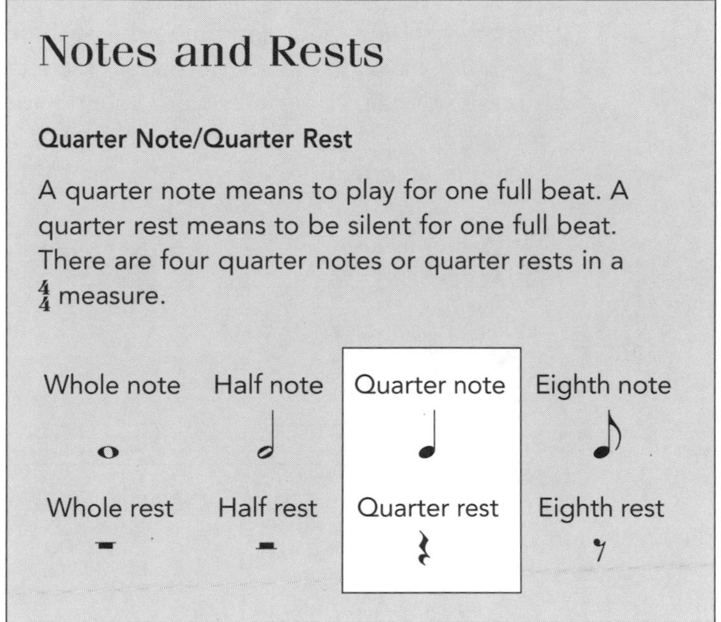

Notes and Rests

Quarter Note/Quarter Rest

A quarter note means to play for one full beat. A quarter rest means to be silent for one full beat. There are four quarter notes or quarter rests in a $\frac{4}{4}$ measure.

Each note should begin with a quick "tu" to help separate it from the others.

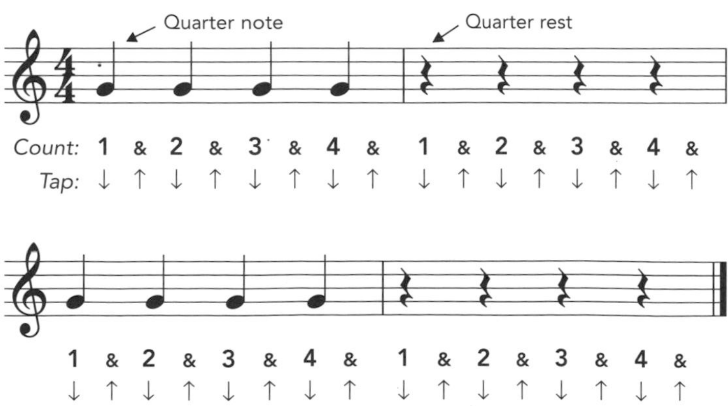

Don't just let the CD play on. Repeat each exercise until you feel comfortable playing it by yourself and with the CD.

A New Note: F

Look for the fingering diagram under each new note. Press down the valves that are colored in. Practicing long tones like this will help to develop your sound and your breath control, so don't just move on to the next exercise. Repeat each one several times.

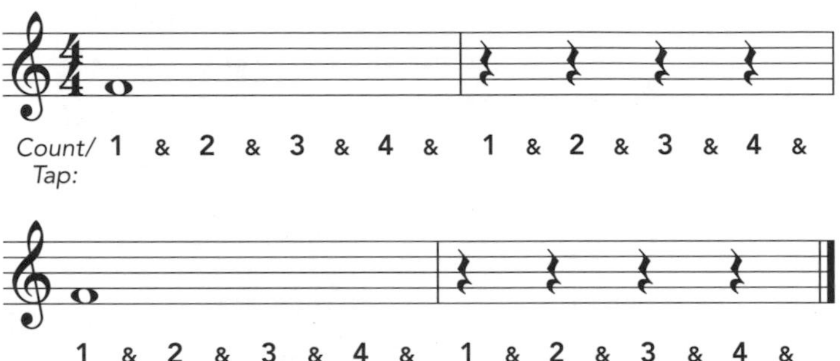

Two's A Team

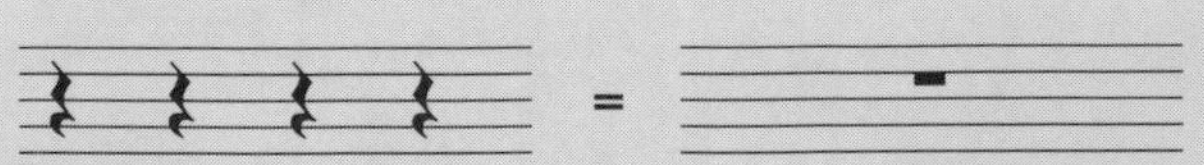

Remember: Rests are silence in music where you play nothing at all. Rests are like notes in that they have their own rhythmic values, instructing you how long (or for how many beats) to pause. Here, four beats of rest can be simplified as a whole rest.

Track 5

A New Note: E

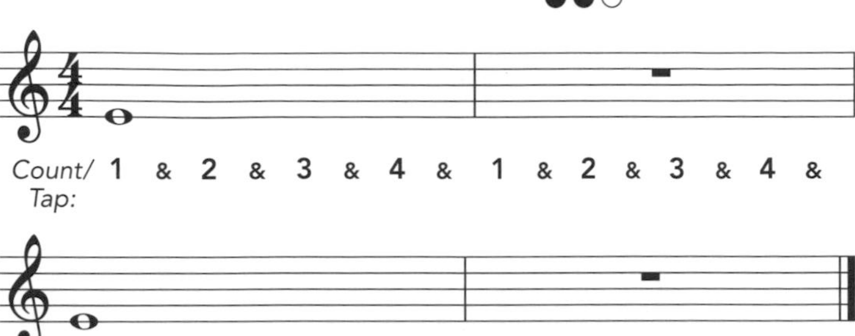

Keeping Time

To keep a steady tempo, try tapping your foot and counting along with each song. In $\frac{4}{4}$ time, tap your foot four times in each measure and count, "1 & 2 & 3 & 4 &." Your foot should touch the floor on the number and come up on the "&." Each number and each "&" should be exactly the same duration, like the ticking of a clock.

Track 6

Moving On Up

If you become winded or your lips get tired, you can still practice by fingering the notes on your instrument and singing the pitches or counting the rhythm out loud.

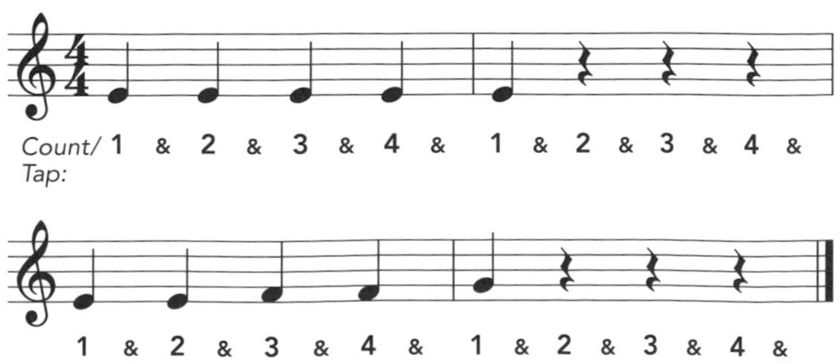

Track 7

A New Note: D

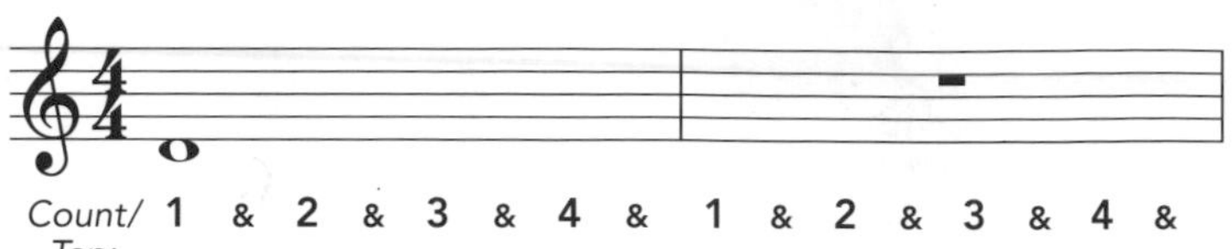

1 & 2 & 3 & 4 & 1 & 2 & 3 & 4 &

Track 8

Four By Four

Repeat Signs

Repeat signs 𝄆 𝄇 tell you to repeat everything between them. If only the sign on the right appears (:‖), repeat from the beginning of the piece.

Track 9

A New Note: C

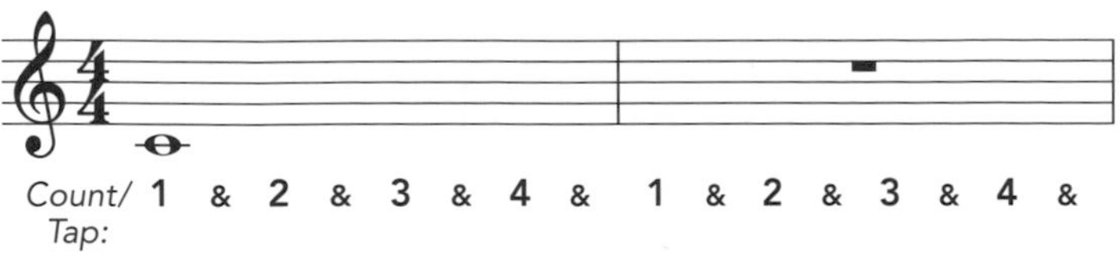

Track 10

The Fab Five

Track 11

First Flight

Keep the beat steady by silently counting or tapping while you play.

Track 12

Rolling Along

Tonguing

To start each note, whisper the syllable "tu." Keep the air stream going continuously and just flick the tip of your tongue against the back of your upper teeth for each new note. If the notes change, be sure to move your fingers quickly so that each note will come out cleanly. When you come to a rest or the end of the song, just stop blowing. Using your tongue to stop the air will cause an abrupt and unpleasant ending of the sound.

Lesson 2

- Play long tones to warm up at the beginning of every practice session.
- Tap, count out loud and sing through each exercise with the CD before you play it.
- Play each exercise several times until you feel comfortable with it.

Track 13

Hot Cross Buns

Notes and Rests

Half Note/Half Rest

A half note means to play for two full beats. (It's equal in length to two quarter notes.) A half rest means to be silent for two beats. There are two half notes or half rests in a $\frac{4}{4}$ measure.

Whole note	Half note	Quarter note	Eighth note
𝅝	𝅗𝅥	♩	♪
Whole rest	**Half rest**	**Quarter rest**	**Eighth rest**
𝄻	𝄼	𝄽	𝄾

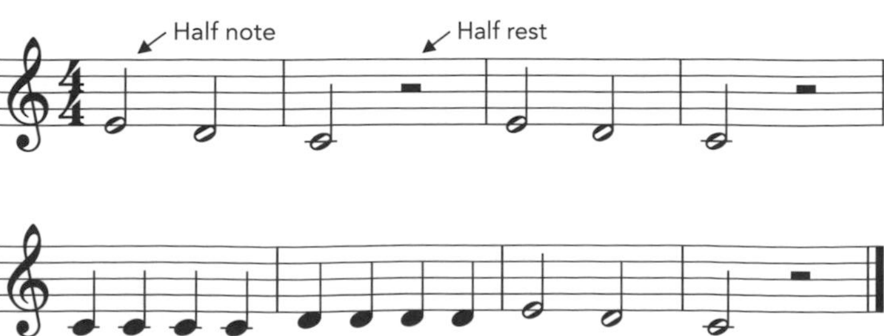

Track 14

Go Tell Aunt Rhodie

Breath Mark

The breath mark (,) indicates a specific place to inhale. Play the proceeding note for the full length then take a deep, quick breath through your mouth.

Make certain that your cheeks don't puff out when you blow.

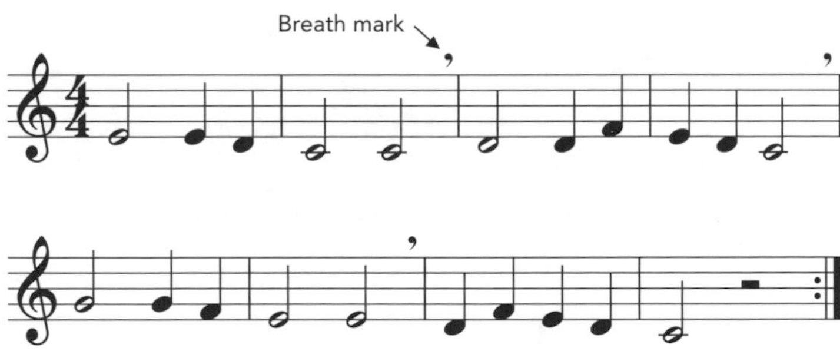

Track 15

The Whole Thing

Remember: a whole rest (-) indicates a whole measure of silence. Note that the whole rest hangs down from the 4th line, whereas the half rest sits on the 3rd line.

Lightly Row

Reaching Higher (New Note: A)

Always practice long tones on each new note.

> ## Fermata
> The fermata (𝄐) indicates that a note or rest is held somewhat longer than normal.

Au Claire De La Lune

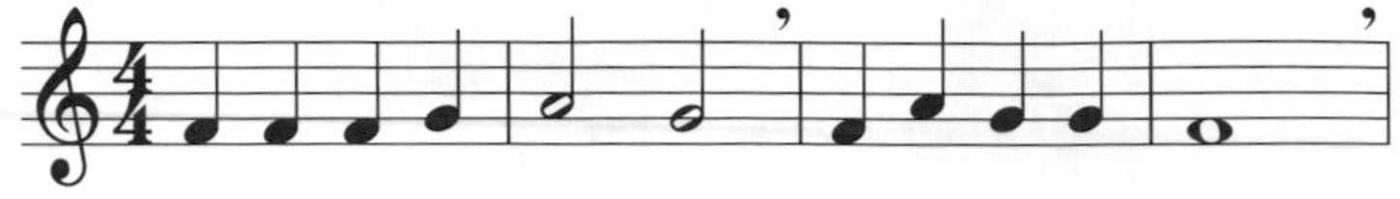

Twinkle, Twinkle Little Star

Lesson 3

Check these points so you will get the best sound from your trumpet.

- If you get a bubbling sound as you play, drain the water from the slides by pressing the water keys as you blow air (without buzzing your lips) through the trumpet. If this doesn't help, pull the slides out individually and empty the water from them.
- Make certain that your cheeks don't puff out when you blow.
- Keep the center section of your lips relaxed at all times.

Deep Pockets (New Note: B)

Always practice long tones on each new note.

Track 21

Doodle All Day

Try to play this on your mouthpiece only before you play it on your trumpet.

Breath Support

In order to play in tune and with a full, beautiful tone, it is necessary to breathe properly and control the air as you play. Quickly take the breath in through your mouth all the way to the bottom of your lungs. Then tighten your stomach muscles and push the air quickly through the trumpet, controlling the air with your lips. Practice this by forming your lips as you do when you play and then blowing against your hand. If the air is cool, you are doing it correctly. If the air is warm, tighten the lips and make the air stream smaller. Keep the air stream moving fast at all times, especially as you begin to run out of air. Practice blowing against your hand and see how long you can keep the air going. Work to keep the air stream cool and steady from beginning to end.

Now try this with your trumpet. Select a note that is comfortable to play and see how long you can hold it. Listen carefully to yourself to see if the tone gets louder or softer, changes pitch slightly, or if the quality of the tone changes. Do this a few times every time you practice, trying to hold the note a little longer each time and maintain a good sound.

Jingle Bells

Dynamics

Dynamics refer to how loud or soft the music is. Traditionally, many musical terms (including dynamic markings) are called by their Italian names:

f	forte *(four' tay)*	loud
mf	mezzo forte *(met' zoh four' tay)*	moderately loud
p	piano *(pee ahn' oh)*	soft

Producing a louder sound requires more air, but you should use full breath support at all dynamic levels.

My Dreydl

Pick-up Notes

Sometimes there are notes that come before the first full measure. They are called ***pick-up notes***. Often, when a song begins with a pick-up measure, the note's value (in beats) is subtracted from the last measure. To play this song with a one beat pick-up, you count "1, 2, 3" and start playing on beat 4.

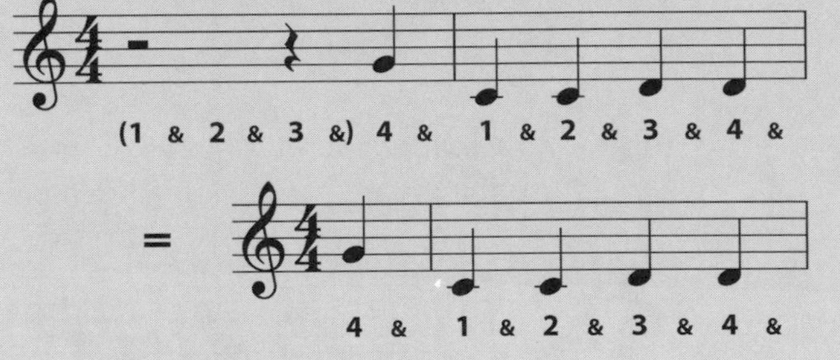

Eighth Note Jam

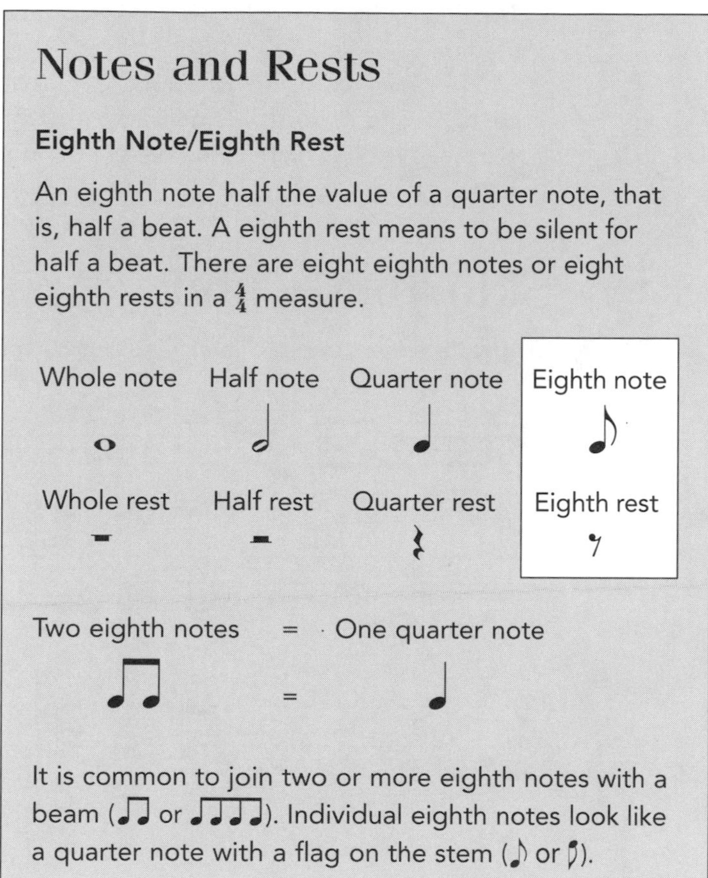

Notes and Rests

Eighth Note/Eighth Rest

An eighth note half the value of a quarter note, that is, half a beat. A eighth rest means to be silent for half a beat. There are eight eighth notes or eight eighth rests in a $\frac{4}{4}$ measure.

It is common to join two or more eighth notes with a beam (♫ or ♬♬). Individual eighth notes look like a quarter note with a flag on the stem (♪ or ♪).

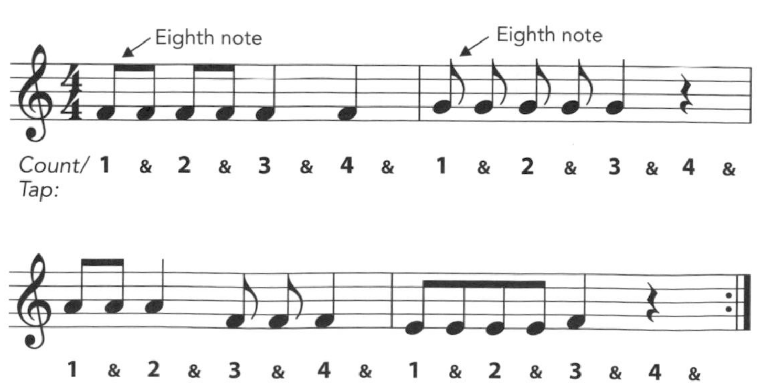

Eighth Note Counting

The first eighth note comes on "1" as your foot taps the floor. The second happens as your foot moves up on "&." The third is on "2" and the fourth is on the next "&" and so forth. Remember to count and tap in a steady and even manner, like the ticking of a clock.

Track 25

Skip To My Lou

Keep your fingers close to the valves and curved comfortably.

Track 26

Oh, Susanna

Notice the pick-up notes.

William Tell

Good posture will improve your sound.

Lesson 4

- Support the trumpet with your left hand, leaving the fingers of your right hand free to move.
- Be sure to blow enough air through your trumpet for a smooth, even sound. Be careful not to blow too hard or to "blast" your tone.

Two By Two

$\frac{2}{4}$ Time

A time signature of $\frac{2}{4}$ means that a quarter note gets one beat, but there are only two beats in a measure.

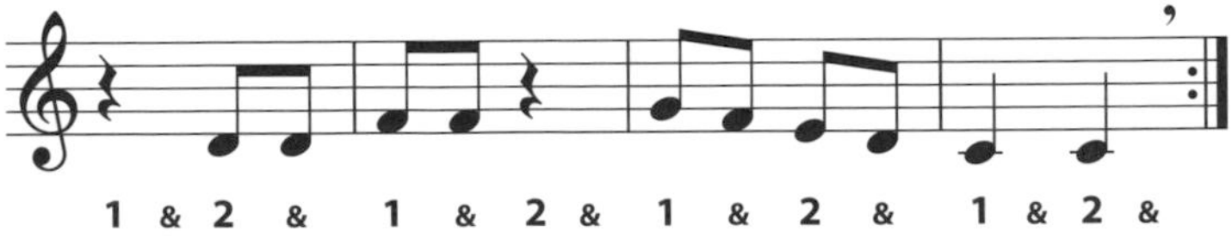

High School Cadets March

Tempo Markings

The speed or pace of music is called t***empo***. Tempo markings are usually written above the staff. Many of these terms come from the Italian.

Allegro *(ah lay' grow)* Fast tempo

Moderato *(mah der ah' tow)* Medium or moderate tempo

Andante *(ahn dahn' tay)* Slower "walking" tempo

Hey, Ho! Nobody's Home

(New Note: A)

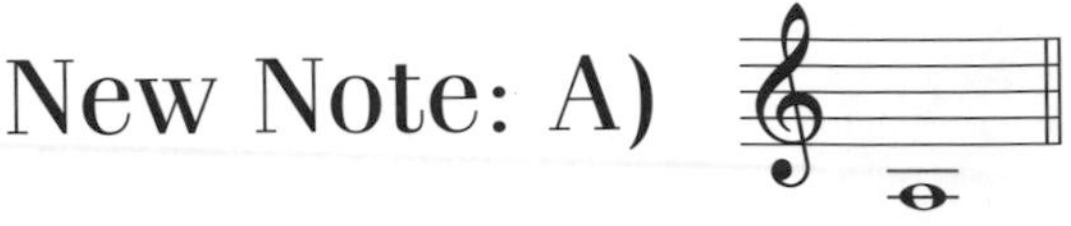

Octaves

Notes that have the same name but are eight notes higher or lower are called ***octaves***. You already knew how to play an A, but this new A is one octave lower. Practice playing both A's one after the other like this:

The higher notes will be played more easily if you:

- With your lips, make the air stream round rather than flat.
- Move your jaw slightly forward so the high stream is directed a little higher.
- Blow the air slightly faster.

Track 31

Play The Dynamics

Dynamics

Gradual changes in volume are indicated by these symbols:

< ***Crescendo*** (gradually louder) sometimes abbreviated *cresc.*

> ***Decrescendo*** or ***Diminuendo*** (gradually softer) sometimes abbreviated *dim.*

Remember to keep the air stream moving fast both as you get louder by gradually using more air on the crescendo, and as you get softer by gradually using less air on the decrescendo.

Track 32

Frère Jacques

Track 33

Hard Rock Blues

Posture

Good body posture will allow you to take in a full, deep breath and control the air better as you play. Sit or stand with your spine straight and tall. Your shoulders should be back and relaxed. Keep your jaw parallel to the floor and don't let your right arm drop down. Think about your posture as you begin playing and check it several times while playing.

Lesson 5

Alouette

Tie

A ***tie*** is a curved line connecting two notes of the same pitch. It indicates that instead of playing both notes, you play the first note and hold it for the total time value of both notes.

 = 2 beats

Dot

A ***dot*** adds half the value of the note to which it is attached. A dotted half note (𝅗𝅥.) has a total time value of three beats:

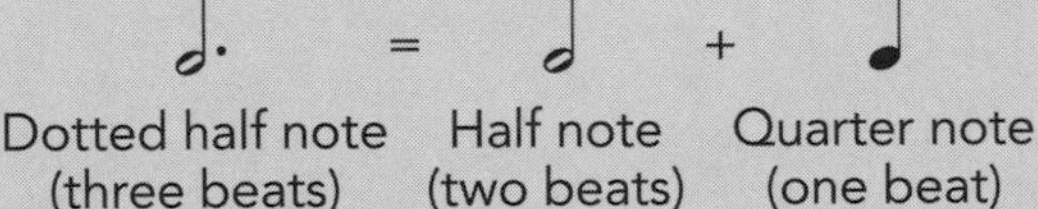

Dotted half note (three beats) | Half note (two beats) | Quarter note (one beat)

Therefore, a dotted half note has exactly the same value as a half note tied to a quarter note. Playing track 34 again, compare this music to the previous example:

Track 35

Camptown Races

Always use a full air stream. Keep your fingers resting on top of the valves, arched naturally.

Track 36

The Nobles

Notice the tie across the bar line between the first and second measure. The G on the third beat is held through the following beats 4 and 1.

Three Beat Jam

$\frac{3}{4}$ Time

The next song is in $\frac{3}{4}$ time signature. That is, three beats (quarter notes) per measure.

$\frac{3}{4}$ time feels very different from $\frac{4}{4}$ time. Putting more emphasis on the first beat of each measure will help you feel the new meter.

Morning (from Peer Gynt)

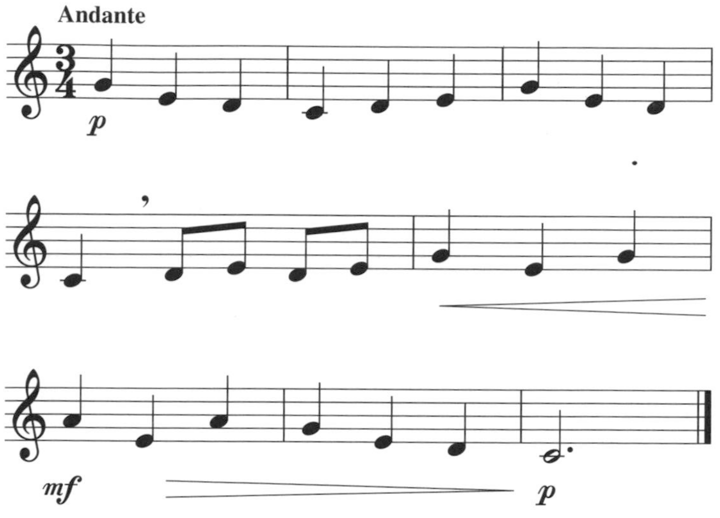

Hand and Finger Position

Now is a good time to go back to page 8 and review proper hand and finger position. This is very important to proper technique. Keeping the fingers curved over the valves will allow your fingers and hands to be relaxed and will aid in getting from one note to another quickly, easily, and accurately. Remember to rest the top of your fingers on the valves and to let your left hand support the weight of the instrument.

Lesson 6

- As you finger the notes on your trumpet, you can practice quietly by speaking the names of the notes, counting out the rhythms, or singing or whistling the pitches, or buzzing on the mouthpiece after removing it from the trumpet.
- Don't let your cheeks puff out when you play.
- Keep the center section of your lips relaxed at all times.
- Use plenty of air and keep it moving ***through*** the instrument.

Track 39

Mexican Clapping Song ("Chiapanecas")

Accent

The accent (>) means you should emphasize the note to which it is attached. Do this by using a more explosive "t" on the "tu" with which you produce the note.

Hot Muffins (New Note: B♭)

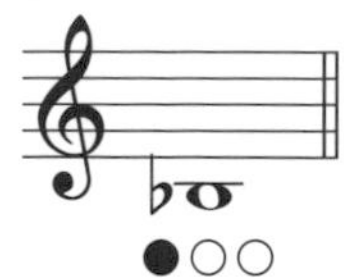

Sharps, Flats, and Naturals

Any sharp (♯), flat (♭), or natural (♮) sign that appears in the music but is not in the key signature is called an ***accidental***. The accidental in the next example is a B♭ and it effects all of the B's for the rest of the measure.

A **sharp** (♯) raises the pitch of a note by one half step.

A **flat** (♭) lowers the pitch of a note by one half step.

A **natural** (♮) cancels a previous sharp or flat, returning a note to its original pitch.

When a song requires a note to be a half step higher or lower, you'll see a sharp (♯), flat (♭), or natural (♮) sign in front of it. This tells you to raise or lower the note *for that measure only.* We'll see more of these "accidentals" as we continue learning more notes on the trumpet.

Cossack Dance

Notice the repeat sign at the end of the fourth measure. Although this particular repeat sign does not occur at the end of the exercise, it behaves just like any other repeat sign. Play the repeated section twice, then continue.

Basic Blues (New Note: B♭)

For higher notes, don't press the mouthpiece hard against your lips. Instead, follow these suggestions:

- Firm the corners of your mouth.
- Raise the back of your tongue slightly, as if whispering "tee."
- Blow the air slightly faster through your instrument.

Track 43

High Flying

Key Signature – F

The ***key signature*** tells which notes are played as sharps or flats throughout the entire piece. Until now, all of the exercises have been written in the ***Key of C***, which has no sharps or flats. This exercise introduces a new key signature: the ***Key of F***. Play B♭ throughout the piece.

1st and 2nd Endings

The use of ***1st and 2nd endings*** is a variant on the basic repeat sign. You play through the music to the repeat sign and repeat as always, but the second time through the music, skip the measure or measures under the "first ending" and go directly to the "second ending."

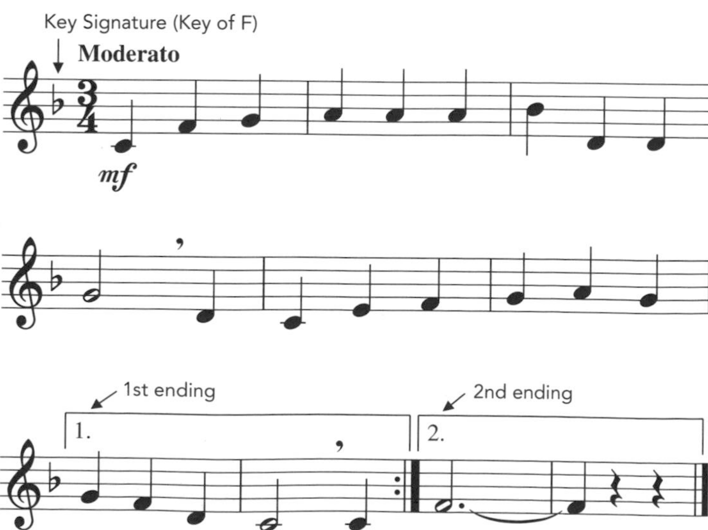

Up On A Housetop

Lesson 7

The Big Airstream

(New Note: C)

Waltz Theme

Track 47

Down By The Station

Track 48s

Banana Boat Song

D.C. al Fine

At the ***D.C. al Fine***, play again from the beginning, stopping at ***Fine***. D.C. is the abbreviation for Da Capo (dah cah' poh), which means "to the beginning." Fine (fee' neh) means "the end."

Always check the key signature.

Lesson 8

Razor's Edge (New Note: F♯)

Sharp Sign

A sharp sign (♯) raises the pitch of a note by a half-step for the remainder of the measure.

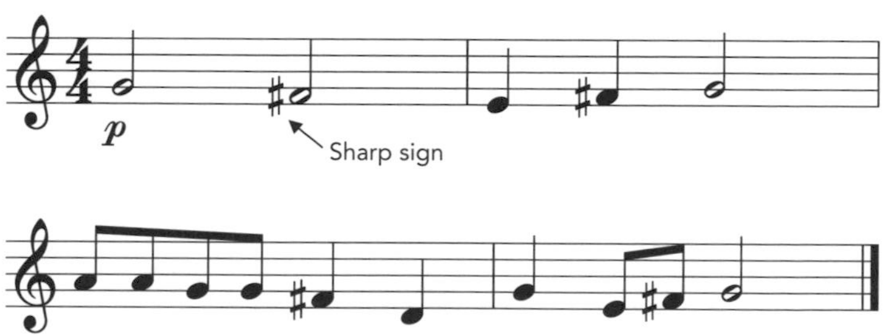

The Music Box

Smooth Operator

Slur

A curved line connecting notes of different pitch is called a ***slur***. Notice the difference between a slur and a tie, which connects notes of the ***same*** pitch.

Only tongue the first note of a slur. As you finger the next note, keep the breath going.

Gliding Along

This exercise is almost identical to the previous one. Notice how the different slurs change the tonguing.

Track 53

Take The Lead (New Note: B)

Track 54

The Cold Wind

Phrase

A phrase is a musical "sentence," often 2 or 4 measures long. Try to play a phrase in one breath.

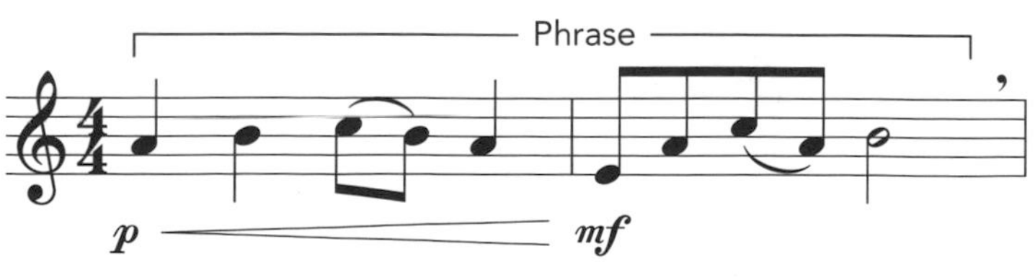

Track 55

Satin Latin

Key Signature – G

A key signature with one sharp indicates that all written F's should be played as F♯'s. This is the ***Key of G***.

Multiple Measure Rest

Sometimes you won't play for several measures. The number above the ***multiple measure rest*** (⊢⊣) indicates how many full measures to rest. Count through the silent measures.

Track 56

Naturally

Natural Sign

A natural sign (♮) cancels a flat or a sharp for the remainder of the measure.

Track 57

The Flat Zone (New Note: E♭)

Check the key signature

Track 58

On Top Of Old Smokey

Track 59

All Through The Night

Dotted Quarter Note

Remember that a dot adds half the value of the note. A dotted quarter note followed by a eighth note (♩. ♪) and (♩‿♪♪) have the same rhythmic value.

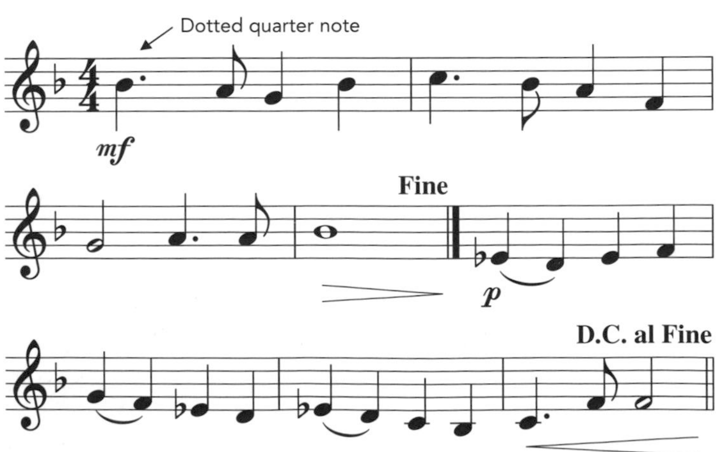

Track 60

Sea Chanty

Always use a full air stream.

Track 61

Scarborough Fair

Track 62

Auld Lang Syne

Lesson 10

Notes that are slurred without changing the fingering are called ***lip slurs***. Brass players practice lip slurs to develop a stronger air stream and embouchure, and to increase range. You should practice lip slurs every day. To play lip slurs well:

- Keep your throat as open and relaxed as possible. If your throat is tense, imagine that you are yawning as you play.
- While playing the first note of a lip slur, *think* the pitch of the slurred note *before* you play it.
- Keep the air stream full and steady to the end of the slur. This doesn't mean that you should play loudly, but that you should support the tone with your breath.

Track 63

Slur Exercise No. 1 (Lip Slur)

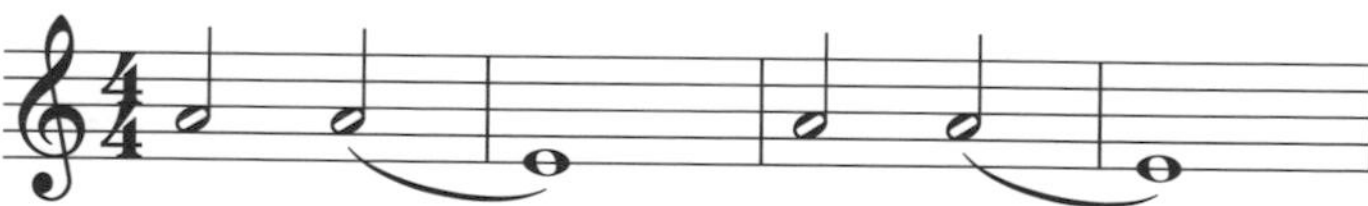

Track 64

Slur Exercise No. 2

Slur Exercise No. 3 (Lip Slur)

Technique Trax

Stepping Stones (New Note: D)

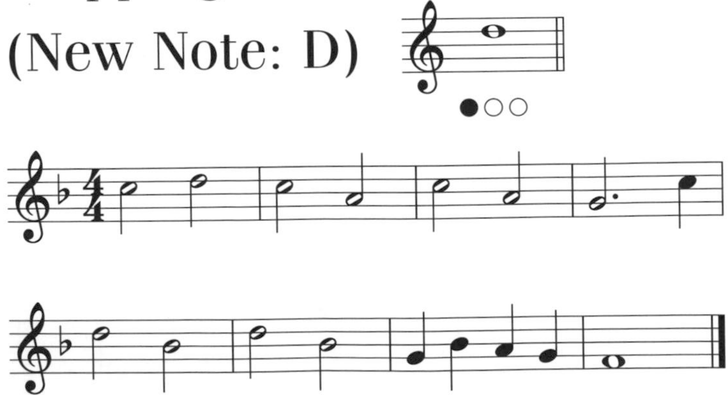

Austrian Waltz

Lesson 11

Michael Row The Boat Ashore

Repeat the section of music enclosed by the repeat signs (‖: :‖). If 1st and 2nd endings are used, they are played as usual—but go back only to the first repeat sign, not to the beginning.

Finlandia

C Time Signature

Common time (C) is the same as $\frac{4}{4}$.

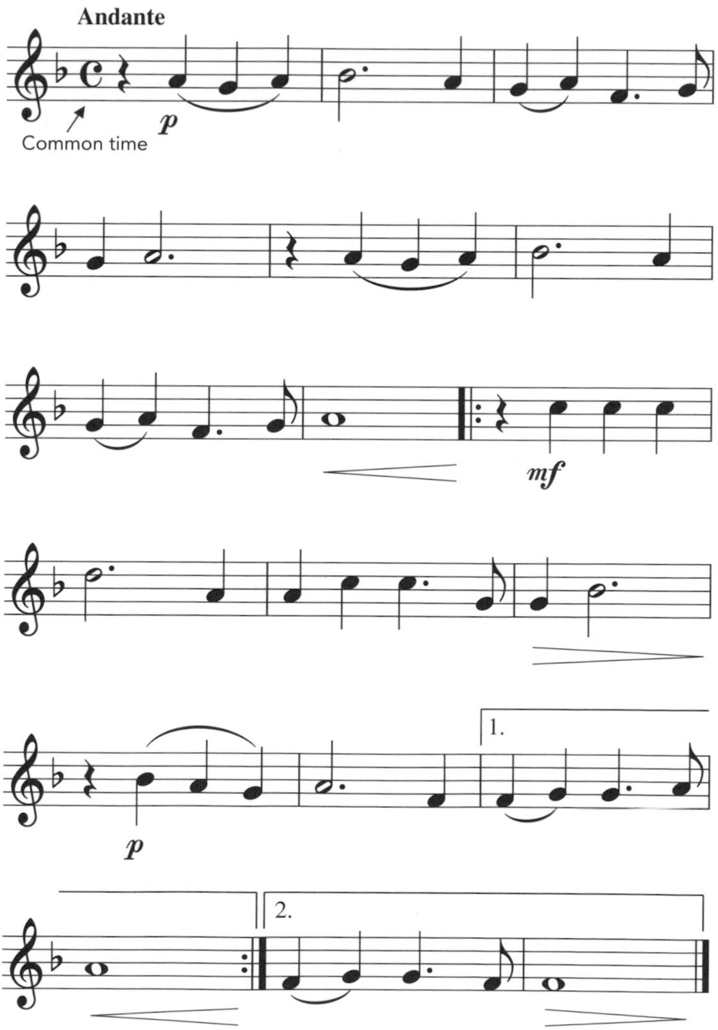

Andante

Common time

p

mf

p

1.

2.

When The Saints Go Marching In

Allegro

f

1.

2.

Track 72

Botany Bay

Track 73

The Streets of Laredo

Trumpet Scales and Arpeggios

Key of C

Trumpet Scales and Arpeggios

Key of F

Trumpet Scales and Arpeggios

Key of G

Trumpet Scales and Arpeggios

Key of B♭

Play all B's as B-flat and all E's as E-flat.

Bonus Songs

Forrest Gump – Main Title

(Feather Theme)

from the Paramount Motion Picture FORREST GUMP

Music by ALAN SILVESTRI

Gently

2

mf

f
mf
4
p

We Will Rock You

Words and Music by BRIAN MAY

Heavy Rock

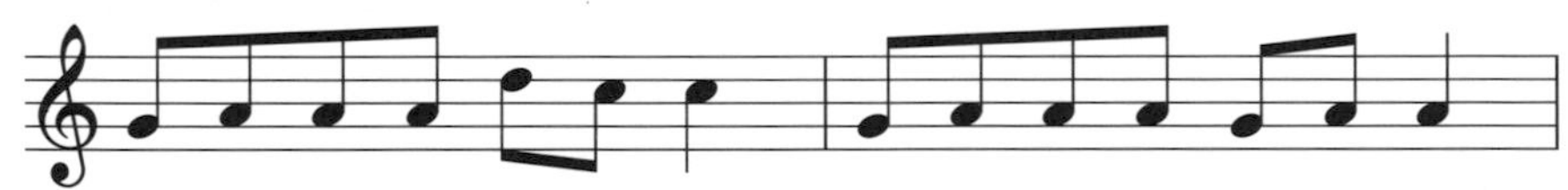

mf
f
mf
f
2
f
ff

The Man From Snowy River

(Main Title Theme)

from THE MAN FROM SNOWY RIVER

By BRUCE ROWLAND

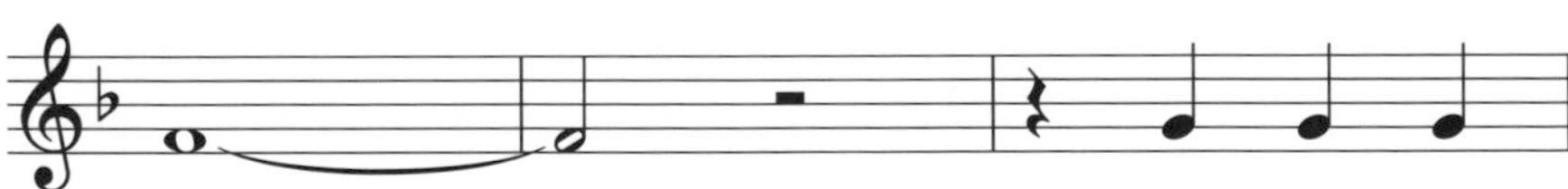

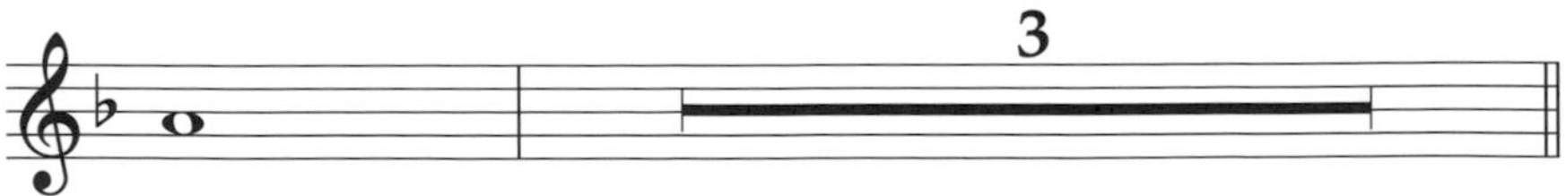

f
mf
2
f

Track 74

Chariots Of Fire

from CHARIOTS OF FIRE

Music by VANGELIS

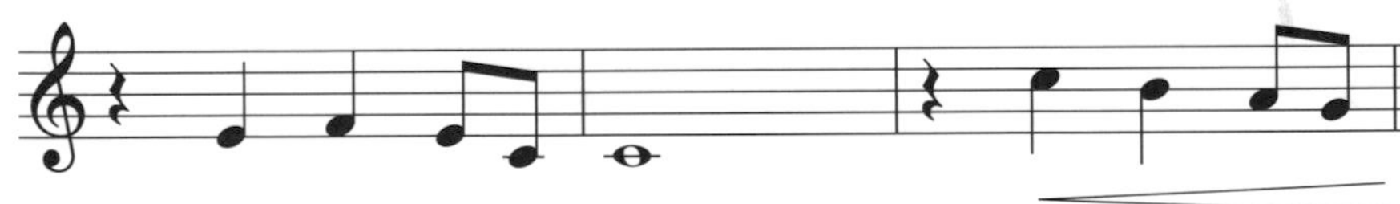

mf
f
mf
f

Rock & Roll – Part II

(The Hey Song)

Words and Music by
MIKE LEANDER and GARY GLITTER

Steady Rock Shuffle (♫ = ♩ ♪)

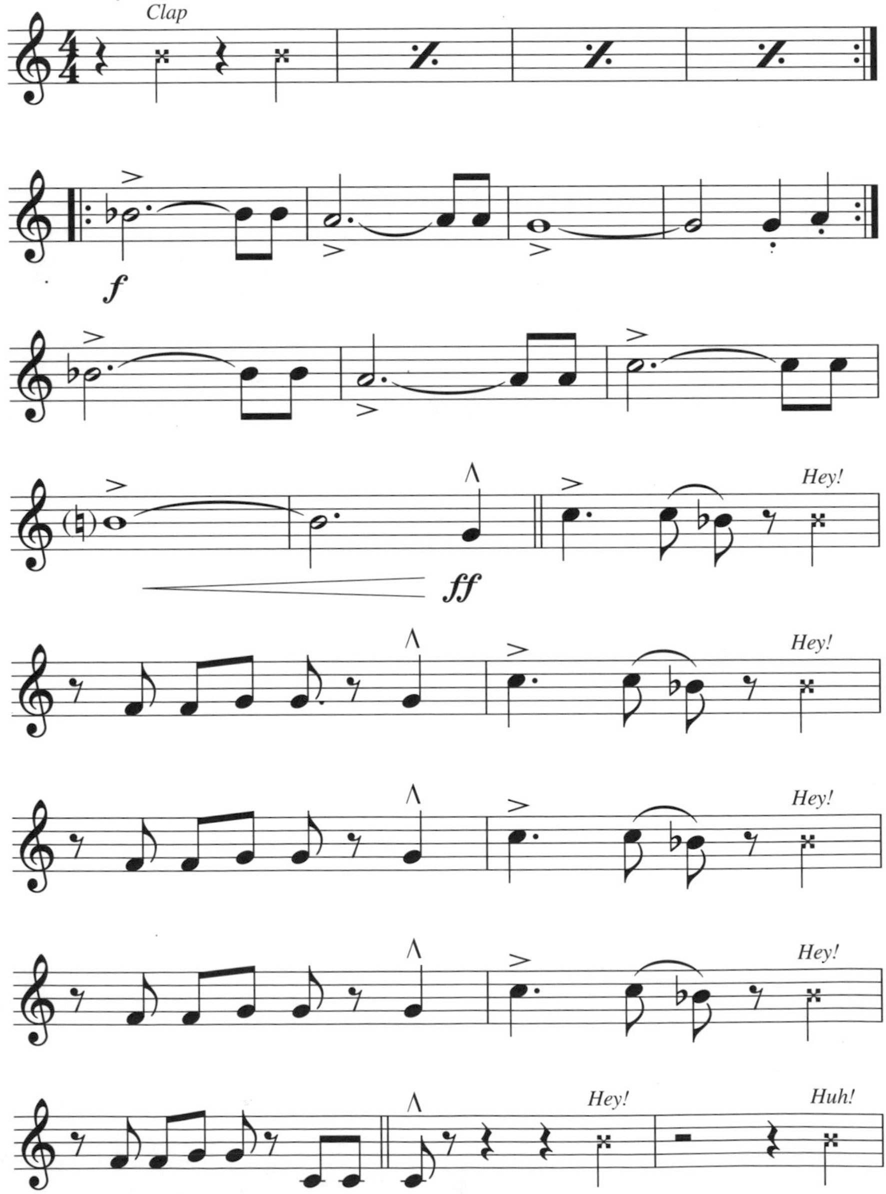

Clap

f

ff

Hey!

Hey!

Hey!

Hey!

Hey!

Huh!

Hey!
Huh!
Hey!
Huh!
Hey!
ff
Hey!
Hey!
Hey!
Hey!

Fingering Chart for Trumpet

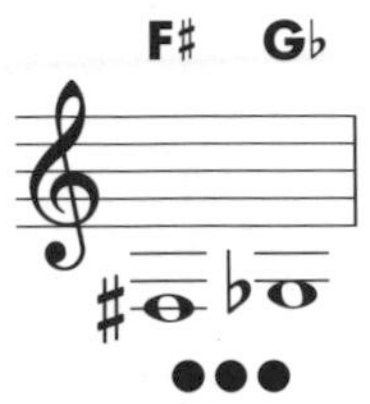

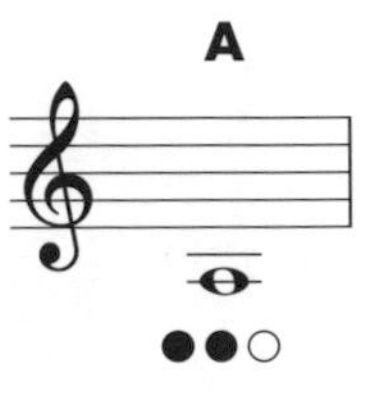

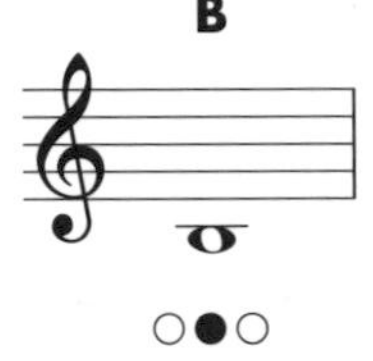

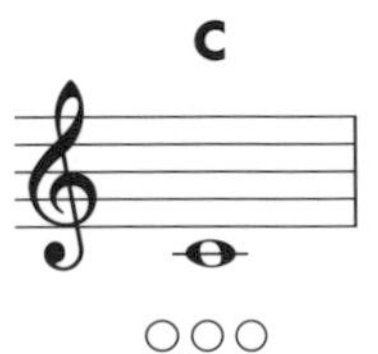

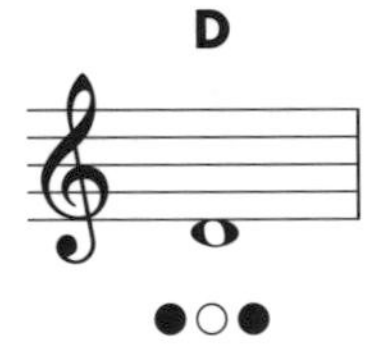

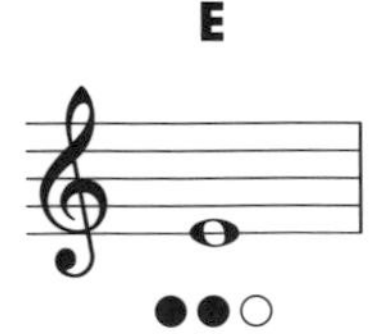

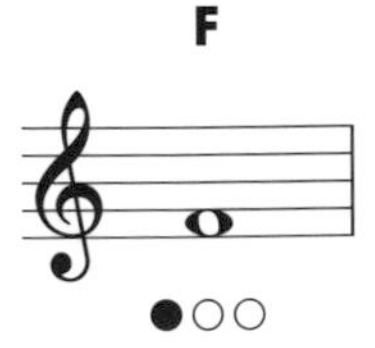

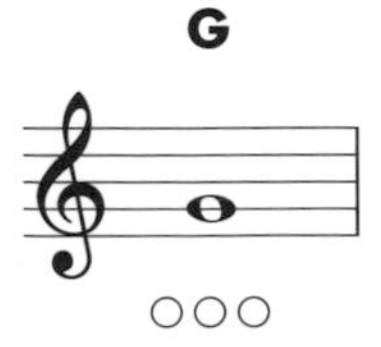

Fingering Chart for Trumpet

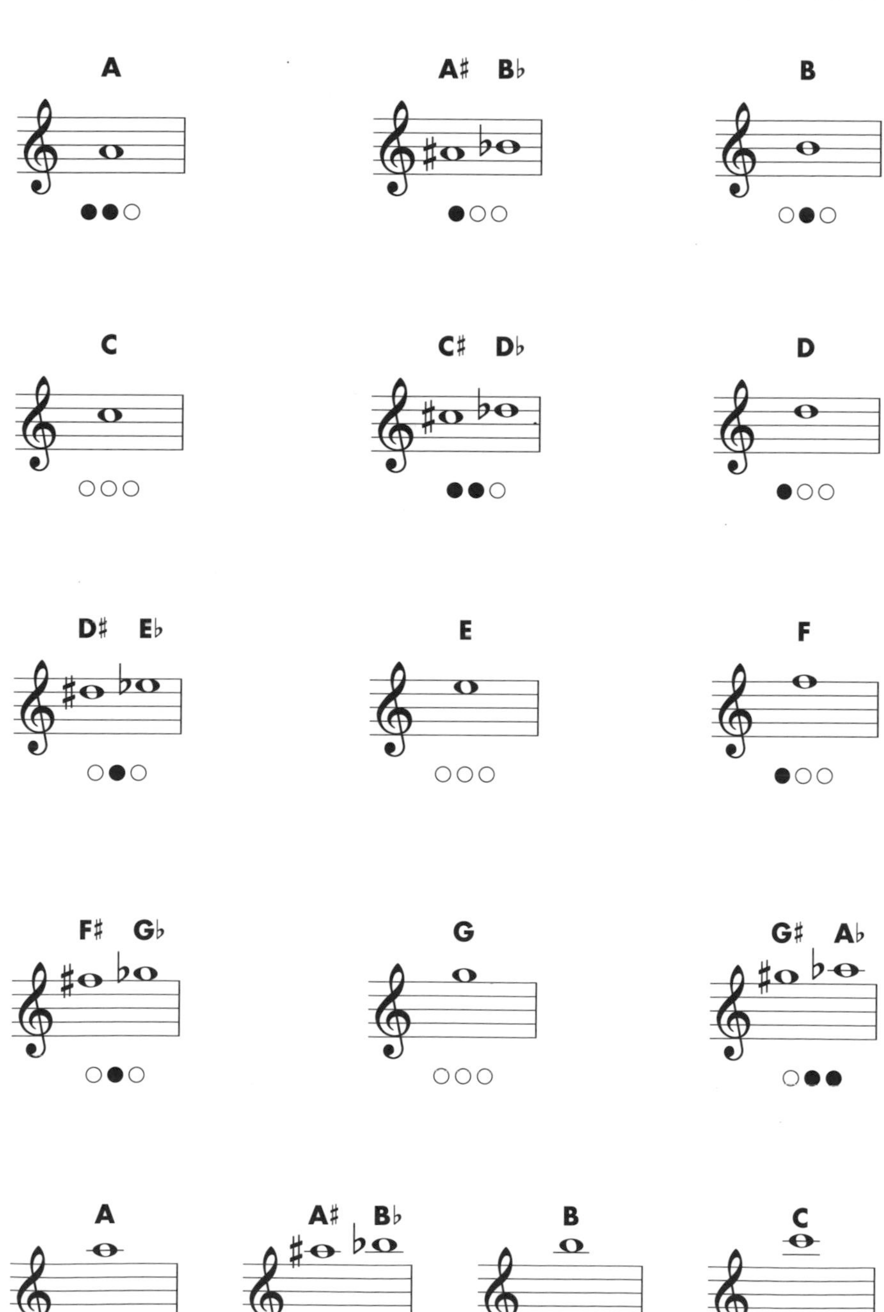

Glossary of Musical Terms

Accent	An Accent mark (>) means you should emphasize the note to which it is attached.
Accidental	Any sharp (♯), flat (♭), or natural (♮) sign that appears in the music but is not in the key signature is called an Accidental.
Allegro	Fast tempo.
Andante	Slower "walking" tempo.
Arpeggio	An Arpeggio is a "broken" chord whose notes are played individually.
Bass Clef (𝄢)	(F Clef) indicates the position of note names on a music staff: The fourth line in Bass Clef is F.
Bar Lines	Bar Lines divide the music staff into measures.
Beat	The Beat is the pulse of music, and like a heartbeat it should remain very steady. Counting aloud and foot-tapping help maintain a steady beat.
Breath Mark	The Breath Mark (,) indicates a specific place to inhale. Play the proceeding note for the full length then take a deep, quick breath through your mouth.
Chord	When two or more notes are played together, they form a Chord or harmony.
Chromatic Notes	Chromatic Notes are altered with sharps, flats and natural signs which are not in the key signature.
Chromatic Scale	The smallest distance between two notes is a half-step, and a scale made up of consecutive half-steps is called a Chromatic Scale.
Common Time	Common Time (𝄴) is the same as $\frac{4}{4}$ time signature.
Crescendo	Play gradually louder. (*cresc.*)
D.C. al Fine	D.C. al Fine means to play again from the beginning, stopping at Fine. D.C. is the abbreviation for Da Capo, or "to the beginning," and Fine means "the end."
Decrescendo	Play gradually softer. (*decresc.*)
Diminuendo	Same as decrescendo. (*dim.*)

Dotted Half Note	A note three beats long in duration (𝅗𝅥.). A dot adds half the value of the note.
Dotted Quarter Note	A note one and a half beats long in duration (♩.). A dot adds half the value of the note.
Double Bar (‖)	Indicates the end of a piece of music.
Duet	A composition with two different parts played together.
Dynamics	Dynamics indicate how loud or soft to play a passage of music. Remember to use full breath support to control your tone at all dynamic levels.
Eighth Note	An Eighth Note (♪) receives half the value of a quarter note, that is, half a beat. Two or more eighth notes are usually joined together with a beam, like this: ♫
Eighth Rest	Indicates 1/2 beat of silence. (𝄾)
Embouchure	Your mouth's position on the mouthpiece of the instrument.
Enharmonics	Two notes that are written differently, but sound the same (and played with the same fingering) are called Enharmonics.
Fermata	The Fermata (𝄐) indicates that a note (or rest) is held somewhat longer than normal.
1st & 2nd Endings	The use of 1st and 2nd Endings is a variant on the basic repeat sign. You play through the music to the repeat sign and repeat as always, but the second time through the music, skip the measure or measures under the "first ending" and go directly to the "second ending."
Flat (♭)	Lowers the note a half step and remains in effect for the entire measure.
Forte (*f*)	Play loudly.
Half Note	A Half Note (𝅗𝅥) receives two beats. It's equal in length to two quarter notes.
Half Rest	The Half Rest (𝄼) marks two beats of silence.

Glossary continued

Harmony	Two or more notes played together. Each combination forms a chord.
Interval	The distance between two pitches is an Interval.
Key Signature	A Key Signature (the group of sharps or flats before the time signature) tells which notes are played as sharps or flats throughout the entire piece.
Largo	Play very slow.
Ledger Lines	Ledger Lines extend the music staff. Notes on ledger lines can be above or below the staff.
Mezzo Forte (*mf*)	Play moderately loud.
Mezzo Piano (*mp*)	Play moderately soft.
Moderato	Medium or moderate tempo.
Multiple Measure Rest	The number above the staff tells you how many full measures to rest. Count each measure of rest in sequence. (𝄩)
Music Staff	The Music Staff has 5 lines and 4 spaces where notes and rests are written.
Natural Sign (♮)	Cancels a flat (♭) or sharp (♯) and remains in effect for the entire measure.
Notes	Notes tell us how high or low to play by their placement on a line or space of the music staff, and how long to play by their shape.
Phrase	A Phrase is a musical "sentence," often 2 or 4 measures long.
Piano (*p*)	Play soft.
Pitch	The highness or lowness of a note which is indicated by the horizontal placement of the note on the music staff.
Pick-Up Notes	One or more notes that come before the first full measure. The beats of Pick-Up Notes are subtracted from the last measure.
Quarter Note	A Quarter Note (♩) receives one beat. There are 4 quarter notes in a $\frac{4}{4}$ measure.

Quarter Rest	The Quarter Rest (𝄽) marks one beat of silence.
Repeat Sign	The Repeat Sign (:‖) means to play once again from the beginning without pause. Repeat the section of music enclosed by the repeat signs (‖: :‖). If 1st and 2nd endings are used, they are played as usual—but go back only to the first repeat sign, not to the beginning.
Rests	Rests tell us to count silent beats.
Rhythm	Rhythm refers to how long, or for how many beats a note lasts.
Scale	A Scale is a sequence of notes in ascending or descending order. Like a musical "ladder," each step is the next consecutive note in the key signature.
Sharp (♯)	Raises the note a half step and remains in effect for the entire measure.
Slur	A curved line connecting notes of different pitch is called a Slur.
Tempo	Tempo is the speed of music.
Tempo Markings	Tempo Markings are usually written above the staff, in Italian. (Allegro, Moderato, Andante)
Tie	A Tie is a curved line connecting two notes of the same pitch. It indicates that instead of playing both notes, you play the first note and hold it for the total time value of both notes.
Time Signature	Indicates how many beats per measure and what kind of note gets one beat.
Treble Clef (𝄞)	(G Clef) indicates the position of note names on a music staff: The second line in Treble Clef is G.
Trio	A Trio is a composition with three parts played together.
Whole Note	A Whole Note (𝅝) lasts for four full beats (a complete measure in $\frac{4}{4}$ time).
Whole Rest	The Whole Rest (𝄻) indicates a whole measure of silence.